DESERT SONGS

Selections from the Psalms

Text copyright © 1985 by Thomas Nelson, Inc., Publishers.
All rights reserved. Written permission must be secured from
the publisher to use or reproduce any part of this book, except
for brief quotations in critical reviews or articles.

Published in Nashville, Tennessee, by Thomas Nelson, Inc.
and distributed in Canada by Lawson Falle, Ltd., Cambridge,
Ontario.

The Scriptures in this book are from the New King James
Version. Copyright © 1979, 1980, 1982, Thomas Nelson, Inc.,
Publishers.

Text selections followed by the initials JB are by Jill Briscoe.
Text selections followed by the initials SB are by Stuart
Briscoe.

Printed in Singapore by Tien Wah Press (pte.) Ltd.

ISBN 0-8407-4152-9

DESERT SONGS

Selections from the Psalms in the New King James Version

**Text by
Jill and Stuart Briscoe**

Thomas Nelson Publishers
Nashville • Camden • New York

He turns a wilderness
into pools of water,
and dry land
into water springs.

Oh, give thanks
to the Lord,
for He is good!
For His mercy
endures forever.

They Cried Out
to the Lord

Oh, give thanks to the LORD,
for He is good!
For His mercy endures forever.
Let the redeemed of the LORD say so,
whom He has redeemed from the hand
of the enemy,
and gathered out of the lands,
from the east and from the west,
from the north and from the south....
Oh, that men would give thanks to the
LORD for His goodness,
and for His wonderful works to the
children of men!
For He satisfies the longing soul,
and fills the hungry soul with goodness.
Those who sat in darkness
and in the shadow of death,
bound in affliction and irons—
because they rebelled against the
words of God,
and despised the counsel of
the Most High,
therefore He brought down their heart
with labor;
they fell down, and there was none to help.
Then they cried out to the LORD
in their trouble,
and He saved them out of their distresses.
He brought them out of darkness and
the shadow of death,
and broke their chains in pieces.
Oh, that men would give thanks to the
LORD for His goodness,
and for His wonderful works to the
children of men!
For He has broken the gates of bronze,
and cut the bars of iron in two.

*God's love is an active thing. He
does not use pretty words that leave
us desolate. He makes His creation
serve us so we can survive and enjoy
the best things in life. We should
love as God loves, making our
actions count.—SB*

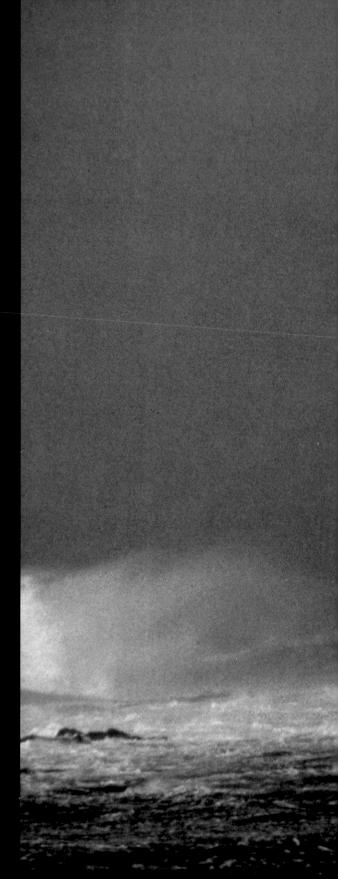

He Stilled the Storm to a Whisper

Fools, because of their transgression,
and because of their iniquities, were afflicted.
Their soul abhorred all manner of food,
and they drew near to the gates of death.
Then they cried out to the LORD in their trouble,
and He saved them out of their distresses.
He sent His word and healed them,
and delivered them from their destructions.
Oh, that men would give thanks to the
LORD for His goodness,
and for His wonderful works
to the children of men!
Let them sacrifice the sacrifices of thanksgiving,
and declare His works with rejoicing.
Those who go down to the sea in ships,
who do business on great waters,
they see the works of the LORD,
and His wonders in the deep.
For he commands and raises the stormy wind,
which lifts up the waves of the sea.
They mount up to the heavens,
they go down again to the depths;
their soul melts because of trouble.
They reel to and fro,
and stagger like a drunken man,
and are at their wits' end.
Then they cry out to the LORD in their trouble,
and He brings them out of their distresses.
He calms the storm,
so that its waves are still.
Then they are glad because they are quiet;
so He guides them to their desired haven.
Oh, that men would give thanks to the
LORD for His goodness,
and for His wonderful works
to the children of men!
Let them exalt Him also in the
congregation of the people,
and praise Him in the assembly of the elders.

*There is a beauty in the desert which is hidden
from the eyes of those who are lost in its
wasteland. There is a richness in the barrenness
of many a life that is unknown to those who
wander apart from You, Lord. Help me show
sunshine and splendor to those who see only
sand and sorrow!*—SB

He Turned the Desert into Pools

He turns rivers into a wilderness,
and the watersprings into dry ground;
a fruitful land into barrenness,
for the wickedness of those who dwell in it.
He turns a wilderness into pools of water,
and dry land into watersprings.
There He makes the hungry dwell,
that they may establish a city for habitation,
and sow fields and plant vineyards,
that they may yield a fruitful harvest.
He also blesses them,
and they multiply greatly;
and He does not let their cattle decrease.
When they are diminished and brought low
through oppression, affliction and sorrow,
He pours contempt on princes,
and causes them to wander in the
wilderness where there is no way;
yet He sets the poor on high,
far from affliction,
and makes their families like a flock.
The righteous see it and rejoice,
and all iniquity stops its mouth.
Whoever is wise will observe these things,
and they will understand the
lovingkindness of the LORD.

I know where I am heading, Lord, for You have promised a safe landfall in glory. But life can be rough and the currents treacherous. So please keep me alert to the fact that You not only await my arrival in port, but You are also on the voyage every inch of the way.—SB

I Will Awaken the Dawn

O God, my heart is steadfast;
I will sing and give praise,
even with my glory.
Awake, lute and harp!
I will awaken the dawn.
I will praise You, O Lord, among the peoples,
and I will sing praises to You among the nations.
For Your mercy is great above the heavens,
and Your truth reaches to the clouds.
Be exalted, O God, above the heavens,
and Your glory above all the earth;
that Your beloved may be delivered,
save with Your right hand, and hear me.
God has spoken in His holiness:
"I will rejoice;
I will divide Shechem
and measure out the Valley of Succoth.
Gilead is Mine; Manasseh is Mine;
Ephraim also is the helmet for My head;
Judah is My lawgiver. Moab is My washpot;
over Edom I will cast My shoe;
over Philistia I will triumph."
Who will bring me into the strong city?
Who will lead me to Edom?
Is it not You, O God, who cast us off?
And You, O God, who did not go out
with our armies?
Give us help from trouble,
for vain is the help of man.
Through God we will do valiantly,
for it is He who shall tread down our enemies.

Sometimes all that my days hold are hostility
and hurt. Rejection and anger meet me at work,
at home, at play. That is why I need to awaken
the dawn and meet Him early if I am to go on
coping; I need to hear how much He loves and
accepts me.—JB

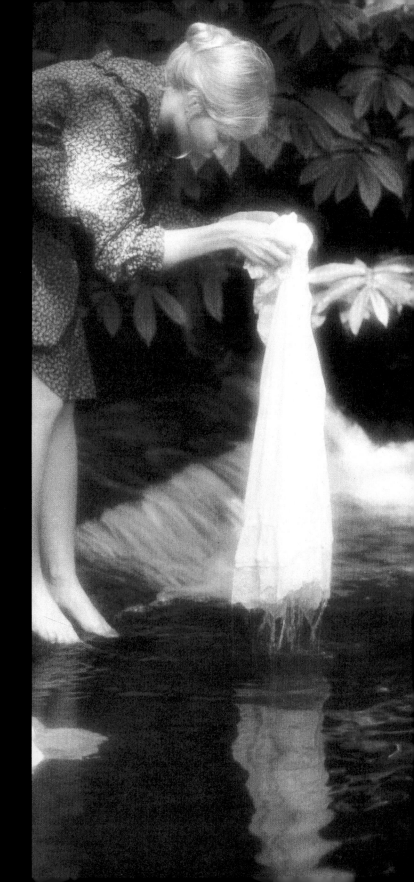

He Wore Cursing as His Garment

Do not keep silent, O God of my praise!
For the mouth of the wicked and the
mouth of the deceitful
have opened against me...
In return for my love they are my accusers,
but I give myself to prayer.
Let his days be few,
and let another take his office.
Let his children be fatherless,
and his wife a widow.
Let his children continually be vagabonds,
and beg;
let them seek their bread also from their
desolate places.
Let the creditor seize all that he has,
and let strangers plunder his labor....
Because he did not remember
to show mercy,
but persecuted the poor and needy man,
that he might even slay
the broken in heart.
As he loved cursing, so let it come to him;
as he did not delight in blessing,
so let it be far from him.
As he clothed himself with cursing as with
his garment,
so let it enter his body like water,
and like oil into his bones.
Let it be to him like the garment which
covers him,
and for a belt with which he girds himself
continually.
Let this be the LORD'S reward to my
accusers,
and to those who speak evil against my
person.

*The dawn announces a new day full
of the promise of divine power for
the tasks that lie ahead. But all too
often I treat new days like
unwelcome intruders or necessary
evils dragging me from the drug of
laziness into the reality of living life.
Teach me to awaken the dawn with
praise, Lord.—SB*

He Stands at the Right Hand of the Needy One

But You, O God the LORD,
deal with me for Your name's sake;
because Your mercy is good, deliver me.
For I am poor and needy,
and my heart is wounded within me.
I am gone like a shadow when it lengthens;
I am shaken off like a locust.
My knees are weak through fasting,
and my flesh is feeble from lack of fatness.
I also have become a reproach to them;
when they look at me,
they shake their heads.
Help me, O LORD my God!
Oh, save me according to Your mercy,
that they may know that this is Your hand—
that You, LORD, have done it!
Let them curse, but You bless;
when they arise, let them be ashamed,
but let Your servant rejoice.
Let my accusers be clothed with shame,
and let them cover themselves with
their own disgrace as with a mantle.
I will greatly praise the LORD with my mouth;
yes, I will praise Him among the multitude.
For He shall stand at the right hand of the poor,
to save him from those who condemn him.

Now that I am grown, I realize I will always be a child; I will always have fears and will always cling to Your protection. I welcome the day, Lord, when You will wrap me in Your arms, shutting out my imaginary harms. —SB

From the Womb of the Dawn

The Lord said to my Lord,
"Sit at My right hand,
till I make Your enemies Your footstool."
The Lord shall send the rod of Your
strength out of Zion.
Rule in the midst of Your enemies!
Your people shall be volunteers
in the day of Your power;
in the beauties of holiness,
from the womb of the morning,
You have the dew of Your youth.
The Lord has sworn and will not relent,
"You are a priest forever according to the order of
Melchizedek."
The Lord is at Your right hand;
He shall execute kings in the day of His wrath.
He shall judge among the nations,
He shall fill the places with dead bodies,
He shall execute the heads of many countries.
He shall drink of the brook by the wayside;
therefore He shall lift up the head.

God brought forth His Son and made Him
prophet, priest, and king. He reigns in Heaven.
It is only a matter of time till all on earth
acknowledge Him. I need not wait till then. I
can bow my knees right now to King Jesus!—JB

*Be exalted, O God,
above the heavens,
and Your glory above
all the earth.*

He Provided Redemption

Praise the LORD!
I will praise the LORD with my whole heart,
in the assembly of the upright and in the
congregation.
The works of the LORD are great,
studied by all who have pleasure in them.
His work is honorable and glorious,
and His righteousness endures forever.
He has made His wonderful works to be
remembered;
the LORD is gracious and full of
compassion.
He has given food to those who fear Him;
He will ever be mindful of His covenant.
He has declared to His people the power of
His works,
in giving them the heritage of the nations.
The works of His hands are verity and
justice;
all His precepts are sure.
They stand fast forever and ever,
and are done in truth and uprightness.
He has sent redemption to His people;
He has commanded His covenant forever:
holy and awesome is His name.
The fear of the LORD is the
beginning of wisdom;
a good understanding have all those who
do His commandments.
His praise endures forever.

Pondering takes time, but it is a
necessary thing. God has given us
"all things richly to enjoy."
Pondering enriches our delight.
Sometimes we can be too spiritually
intense to smell the flowers.—JB

His Children Will Be Mighty

Praise the LORD!
Blessed is the man who fears the LORD,
who delights greatly in His commandments.
His descendants will be mighty on earth;
the generation of the upright will be blessed.
Wealth and riches will be in his house,
and his righteousness endures forever.
Unto the upright there arises light in the darkness;
he is gracious, and full of compassion, and righteous.
A good man deals graciously and lends;
he will guide his affairs with discretion.
Surely he will never be shaken;
the righteous will be in everlasting rememberance.
He will not be afraid of evil tidings;
his heart is steadfast, trusting in the LORD.
His heart is established; he will not be afraid,
until he sees his desire upon his enemies.
He has dispersed abroad, he has given to the poor;
his righteousness endures forever;
his horn will be exalted with honor.
The wicked will see it and be grieved;
he will gnash his teeth and melt away;
the desire of the wicked shall perish.

It is sobering to remember that the way I live affects far more life than I imagine. Little eyes watch me, little minds remember, little instincts mimic, and little people become big persons. Help me to live rightly, not only for Your sake, Lord, but for the sake of the bundle You have placed in my hands. —SB

He Settles the Barren Woman in Her House

Praise the LORD!
Praise, O servants of the LORD,
praise the name of the LORD!
Blessed be the name of the LORD
from this time forth and forevermore!
From the rising of the sun to its going down
The LORD's name is to be praised.
The LORD is high above all nations,
and His glory above the heavens.
Who is like the LORD our God,
who dwells on high,
who humbles Himself to behold
the things that are in the heavens and
in the earth?
He raises the poor out of the dust,
and lifts the needy out of the ash heap,
that He may seat him with princes—
with the princes of His people.
He grants the barren woman a home,
like a joyful mother of children.
Praise the LORD!

How barren the womb that lacks the miracle of conception! How empty the life that knows nothing of the miracle of divine intervention! Lord, bring the light of joy to the eyes of the unknowing as You bring tears of delight to the bearer of children.—JB

The Mountains Skipped like Rams

When Israel went out of Egypt,
the house of Jacob from a people of
strange language,
Judah became His sanctuary,
and Israel His dominion.
The sea saw it and fled; Jordan turned back.
The mountains skipped like rams,
the little hills like lambs.
What ails you, O sea, that you fled?
O Jordan, that you turned back?
O mountains, that you skipped like rams?
O little hills, like lambs?
Tremble, O earth, at the presence of the LORD,
at the presence of the God of Jacob,
who turned the rock into a pool of water,
the flint into a fountain of waters.

*God is working His purposes out. The whole
creation waits for its redemption. Coming out
of Egypt into Canaan will be like waking up in
heaven and hearing the hills sing hallelujah!
One fine day the heavens and earth will be
new.—JB*

He Is Their Help and Shield

Not unto us, O LORD, not unto us,
but to Your name give glory,
because of Your mercy,
and because of Your truth.
Why should the Gentiles say,
"Where now is their God?"
But our God is in heaven;
He does whatever He pleases.
Their idols are silver and gold,
the work of men's hands.
They have mouths, but they do not speak;
eyes they have, but they do not see;
they have ears, but they do not hear;
noses they have, but they do not smell;
they have hands, but they do not handle;
feet they have, but they do not walk;
nor do they mutter through their throat.
Those who make them are like them;
so is everyone who trusts in them....
You who fear the LORD,
trust in the LORD;
He is their help and their shield.
The LORD has been mindful of us;
He will bless us;
He will bless the house of Israel;
He will bless the house of Aaron.
He will bless those who fear the LORD,
both small and great....
The heaven, even the heavens,
are the LORD'S;
but the earth He has given to the children
of men.
The dead do not praise the LORD,
nor any who go down into silence.
But we will bless the LORD
from this time forth and forevermore.
Praise the LORD!

There is awe-inspiring power in the listening ear—God listens. There is great encouragement in the loving look—God sees. There is sweet communion in stimulating talk—God speaks. Idols are dumb because they are dead. God is wise and He is alive. He will be our friend.—JB

The Lord Protects the Simplehearted

I love the LORD, because He has heard
my voice and my supplications.
Because He has inclined His ear to me,
therefore I will call upon Him as long as I live.
The pains of death encompassed me,
and the pangs of Sheol laid hold of me;
I found trouble and sorrow.
Then I called upon the name of the LORD:
"O LORD, I implore You, deliver my soul!"
Gracious is the LORD, and righteous;
yes, our God is merciful.
The LORD preserves the simple;
I was brought low, and He saved me.
Return to your rest, O my soul,
for the LORD has dealt bountifully with you.
For You have delivered my soul from death,
my eyes from tears, and my feet from falling.
I will walk before the LORD in the land of the living.
I believed, therefore I spoke,
"I am greatly afflicted."
I said in my haste, "All men are liars."
What shall I render to the LORD
for all His benefits toward me?
I will take up the cup of salvation,
and call upon the name of the LORD.
I will pay my vows to the LORD
now in the presence of all His people.
Precious in the sight of the LORD
is the death of His saints.
O LORD truly I am Your servant; I am Your servant,
the son of Your maidservant;
You have loosed my bonds.
I will offer to You the sacrifice of thanksgiving,
and will call upon the name of the LORD....
in the courts of the LORD'S house,
in the midst of you, O Jerusalem.
Praise the LORD!

*Dangers lurk on the right hand and on the left,
behind me and before. I need eyes in the back of
my head. Currents unseen and unfelt sweep me
in directions I do not desire—I need strength to
combat them. How thankful I am that You
protect and guide, Lord. Without You my bark
would founder.—SB*

Extol Him, All You Peoples

Oh, praise the LORD, all you Gentiles!
Laud Him, all you peoples!
For His merciful kindness is great
toward us,
and the truth of the LORD endures
forever.
Praise the LORD!

*I am a creature of habit, a servant of tradition.
What people think of me worries me; what they
might say about me binds me like a fetter. But
sometimes the sense of Your grace and glory is
so powerful that my inhibitions disappear like
dew in the sunshine and I praise You and care
for little else.*—SB

He will not allow
your foot to be moved;
He who keeps you
will not slumber.

His Love Endures Forever

Oh, give thanks to the LORD,
for He is good!
Because His mercy endures forever.
Let Israel now say,
"His mercy endures forever."
Let the house of Aaron now say,
"His mercy endures forever."
Let those who fear the LORD now say,
"His mercy endures forever."
I called on the LORD in distress;
the LORD answered me
and set me in a broad place.
The LORD is on my side; I will not fear.
What can man do to me?
The LORD is for me among those who help me;
therefore I shall see my desire on those who hate me.
It is better to trust in the LORD
than to put confidence in man.
It is better to trust in the LORD
than to put confidence in princes.

*Nothing lasts very long these days. Few things
are made very well any more. Quality is in
short demand; quantity seems to be what
matters. Love lasts because God is love and He
endures forever. His love and life can be mine. I
just need to ask!—*JB

He Has Become My Salvation

All nations surrounded me,
but in the name of the LORD I will destroy them.
They surrounded me, yes, they surrounded me;
but in the name of the LORD I will destroy them.
They surrounded me like bees;
they were quenched like a fire of thorns;
for in the name of the LORD I will destroy them.
You pushed me violently, that I might fall,
but the LORD helped me.
The LORD is my strength and song,
and He has become my salvation.
The voice of rejoicing and salvation
is in the tents of the righteous;
the right hand of the LORD does valiantly.
The right hand of the LORD is exalted;
the right hand of the LORD does valiantly.
I shall not die, but live,
and declare the works of the LORD.
The LORD has chastened me severely,
but He has not given me over to death.

God is my strength when I am weak, my song
when I am down, my salvation when I am lost.
God levels with me in love. He loves me too
much to spoil me. He wants me to grow up and
fight His battles for Him.—JB

With Boughs in Hand, Join in the Festal Procession

Open to me the gates of righteousness;
I will go through them, and I will praise the LORD.
This is the gate of the LORD,
through which the righteous shall enter.
I will praise You, for You have answered me,
and have become my salvation.
The stone which the builders rejected
has become the chief cornerstone.
This was the LORD'S doing;
it is marvelous in our eyes.
This is the day which the LORD has made;
we will rejoice and be glad in it.
Save now, I pray, O LORD;
O LORD, I pray, send now prosperity.
Blessed is he who comes in the name
of the LORD!
We have blessed you from the house of
the LORD.
God is the LORD, and He has given us light;
bind the sacrifice with cords to the
horns of the altar.
You are my God, and I will praise You;
You are my God, I will exalt You.
Oh, give thanks to the LORD, for He is good!
For His mercy endures forever.

It is hard to imagine life without trees and mountains, sunsets and vast horizons. But there was such a time or, rather an eternity. It is impossible to think of everything's being gone—of losing that which is familiar. But should heaven and earth pass away, one thing we know: Your love endures forever.—SB

Open My Eyes That I May See

Deal bountifully with Your servant,
that I may live and keep Your word.
Open my eyes, that I may see
wondrous things from Your law.
I am a stranger in the earth;
do not hide Your commandments from me.
My soul breaks with longing
for Your judgments at all times.
You rebuke the proud—the cursed,
who stray from Your commandments.
Remove from me reproach and contempt,
for I have kept Your testimonies.
Princes also sit and speak against me,
but Your servant meditates on Your statutes.
Your testimonies also are my delight
and my counselors.
My soul clings to the dust;
revive me according to Your word.
I have declared my ways,
and You answered me;
teach me Your statutes.
Make me understand the way
of Your precepts;
so shall I meditate on Your
wondrous works.
My soul melts from heaviness;
strengthen me according to Your word.
Remove from me the way of lying,
and grant me Your law graciously.
I have chosen the way of truth;
Your judgments I have laid before me.
I cling to Your testimonies;
O Lord, do not put me to shame!
I will run in the way of Your
commandments,
for You shall enlarge my heart.

*I look at the ocean seeing only
water, missing the mysteries of the
tides. The sun sets and I think only
of things to be done before nightfall,
missing the color and the rhythm of
Your universe. Open my eyes to Your
order, but more importantly, to Your
law that I might live as I ought.*—SB

How Can a Young Man Keep His Way Pure

Blessed are the undefiled in the way,
who walk in the law of the LORD!
Blessed are those who keep His testimonies,
who seek Him with the whole heart!
They also do no iniquity;
they walk in His ways.
You have commanded us
to keep Your precepts diligently.
Oh, that my ways were directed
to keep Your statutes!
Then I would not be ashamed,
when I look into all Your commandments.
I will praise You with uprightness of heart,
when I learn Your righteous judgments.
I will keep Your statutes;
oh, do not forsake me utterly!
How can a young man cleanse his way?
By taking heed according to Your word.
With my whole heart I have sought You;
oh, let me not wander from Your commandments!
Your word I have hidden in my heart,
that I might not sin against You.
Blessed are You, O LORD!
Teach me Your statutes.
With my lips I have delcared
all the judgments of Your mouth.
I have rejoiced in the way of Your testimonies,
as much as in all riches.
I will meditate on Your precepts,
and contemplate Your ways.
I will delight myself in Your statutes;
I will not forget Your word.

*The answer to the question of purity is very
simple. God's Word hidden in the heart
becomes a special soldier, coming to our aid
It fights the desires of our flesh, the subtle
seducement of our world and the direct
suggestions of the devil. I need to hide God'
Word in my heart.*—JB

I Have Put My Hope in Your Laws

Teach me, O Lord, the way of Your statutes,
and I shall keep it to the end.
Give me understanding,
and I shall keep Your law;
indeed, I shall observe it with my whole heart.
Make me walk in the path of Your commandments,
for I delight in it.
Incline my heart to Your testimonies,
and not to covetousness.
Turn away my eyes from looking at worthless things,
and revive me in Your way.
Establish Your word to Your servant,
who is devoted to fearing You.
Turn away my reproach which I dread,
for Your judgments are good.
Behold, I long for Your precepts;
revive me in Your righteousness.
Let Your mercies come also to me, O Lord—
Your salvation according to Your word.
So shall I have an answer for him who reproaches me,
for I trust in Your word.
And take not the word of truth utterly out of my mouth,
for I have hoped in Your ordinances.
So shall I keep Your law continually,
forever and ever.
And I will walk at liberty, for I seek Your precepts.
I will speak of Your testimonies also before kings,
and will not be ashamed.
And I will delight myself in Your commandments,
which I love.
My hands also I will lift up to Your commandments,
which I love,
and I will meditate on Your statutes.

*The Word of God written by the Spirit of God
helps me understand obedience. Jesus said that
"doing" His sayings shows Him how much I
really love Him. Keeping His commandments
means first grasping the meaning of them.—JB*

The Earth Is Filled with Your Love

Remember the word to Your servant,
upon which You have caused me to hope.
This is my comfort in my affliction,
for Your word has given me life.
The proud have me in great derision,
yet I do not turn aside from Your law.
I remembered Your judgments of old,
O LORD,
and have comforted myself.
Indignation has taken hold of me
because of the wicked,
who forsake Your law.
Your statutes have been my songs
in the house of my pilgrimage.
I remember Your name in the night,
O LORD, and I keep Your law.
This has become mine,
because I kept Your precepts.
You are my portion, O LORD;
I have said that I would keep Your words.
I entreated Your favor with my whole heart;
be merciful to me according to Your word.
I thought about my ways,
and turned my feet to Your testimonies.
I made haste, and did not delay
to keep Your commandments.
The cords of the wicked have bound me,
but I have not forgotten Your law.
At midnight I will rise to
give thanks to You,
because of Your righteous judgments.
I am a companion of all those who fear You,
and of those who keep Your precepts.
The earth, O LORD, is full of Your mercy;
teach me Your statutes.

*You have filled the earth with light. It tinges
the sky at eventide with indescribably delicate
touches, and it seeps gently into mist-filled
hollows, lending mystery to charm. And when
night falls, the stars and the moon add their
special brand of silvery radiance. But how much
more delightful is the love with which You give
the gift of light.—SB*

I Have Put My Hope in Your Laws

Teach me, O LORD, the way of Your statutes,
and I shall keep it to the end.
Give me understanding,
and I shall keep Your law;
indeed, I shall observe it with my whole heart.
Make me walk in the path of Your commandments,
for I delight in it.
Incline my heart to Your testimonies,
and not to covetousness.
Turn away my eyes from looking at worthless things,
and revive me in Your way.
Establish Your word to Your servant,
who is devoted to fearing You.
Turn away my reproach which I dread,
for Your judgments are good.
Behold, I long for Your precepts;
revive me in Your righteousness.
Let Your mercies come also to me, O LORD—
Your salvation according to Your word.
So shall I have an answer for him who reproaches me,
for I trust in Your word.
And take not the word of truth utterly out of my mouth,
for I have hoped in Your ordinances.
So shall I keep Your law continually,
forever and ever.
And I will walk at liberty, for I seek Your precepts.
I will speak of Your testimonies also before kings,
and will not be ashamed.
And I will delight myself in Your commandments,
which I love.
My hands also I will lift up to Your commandments,
which I love,
and I will meditate on Your statutes.

The Word of God written by the Spirit of God helps me understand obedience. Jesus said that "doing" His sayings shows Him how much I really love Him. Keeping His commandments means first grasping the meaning of them.—JB

The Earth Is Filled with Your Love

Remember the word to Your servant,
upon which You have caused me to hope.
This is my comfort in my affliction,
for Your word has given me life.
The proud have me in great derision,
yet I do not turn aside from Your law.
I remembered Your judgments of old,
O Lord,
and have comforted myself.
Indignation has taken hold of me
because of the wicked,
who forsake Your law.
Your statutes have been my songs
in the house of my pilgrimage.
I remember Your name in the night,
O Lord, and I keep Your law.
This has become mine,
because I kept Your precepts.
You are my portion, O Lord;
I have said that I would keep Your words.
I entreated Your favor with my whole heart;
be merciful to me according to Your word.
I thought about my ways,
and turned my feet to Your testimonies.
I made haste, and did not delay
to keep Your commandments.
The cords of the wicked have bound me,
but I have not forgotten Your law.
At midnight I will rise to
give thanks to You,
because of Your righteous judgments.
I am a companion of all those who fear You,
and of those who keep Your precepts.
The earth, O Lord, is full of Your mercy;
teach me Your statutes.

You have filled the earth with light. It tinges the sky at eventide with indescribably delicate touches, and it seeps gently into mist-filled hollows, lending mystery to charm. And when night falls, the stars and the moon add their special brand of silvery radiance. But how much more delightful is the love with which You give the gift of light.—SB

*The Lord shall preserve
your going out and your coming in
from this time forth,
and even forevermore.*

Your Hands Made Me and Formed Me

You have dealt well with Your servant,
O LORD, according to Your word.
Teach me good judgment and knowledge,
for I believe Your commandments.
Before I was afflicted I went astray,
but now I keep Your word.
You are good, and do good;
teach me Your statutes.
The proud have forged a lie against me,
but I will keep Your precepts with my whole heart.
Their heart is as fat as grease,
but I delight in Your law.
It is good for me that I have been afflicted,
that I may learn Your statutes.
The law of Your mouth is better to me
than thousands of shekels of gold and silver.
Your hands have made me and fashioned me;
give me understanding, that I may
learn Your commandments.
Those who fear You will be glad when they see me,
because I have hoped in Your word.
I know, O LORD, that Your judgments are right,
and that in faithfulness You have
afflicted me.
Let, I pray, Your merciful kindness be
for my comfort,
according to Your word to Your servant.
Let Your tender mercies come to me, that I may live;
for Your law is my delight.
Let the proud be ashamed,
for they treated me wrongfully with falsehood;
but I will meditate on Your precepts.
Let those who fear You turn to me,
those who know Your testimonies.
Let my heart be blameless regarding Your statutes,
that I may not be ashamed.

Some say I just happened but I believe that You made me, Lord. They want me to believe I am an accident, Lord, but You tell me I was made according to design. What did You have in mind when You formed me, Lord? What would You have me be? Teach me and I will do Your will.—SB

Your Faithfulness Continues through All Generations

My soul faints for Your salvation,
but I hope in Your word.
My eyes fail from seeking Your word,
saying, "When will You comfort me?"
For I have become like a wineskin in smoke,
yet I do not forget Your statutes.
How many are the days of Your servant?
When will You execute judgment on
those who persecute me?
The proud have dug pits for me,
which is not according to Your law.
All Your commandments are faithful;
they persecute me wrongfully;
Help me!
They almost made an end of me on earth,
but I did not forsake Your precepts.
Revive me according to Your lovingkindness,
so that I may keep the testimony of Your mouth.
Forever, O LORD,
Your word is settled in heaven.
Your faithfulness endures to all generations;
You established the earth, and it abides.
They continue this day according to
Your ordinances, for all are Your servants.
Unless Your law had been my delight,
I would then have perished in my affliction.
I will never forget Your precepts,
for by them You have given me life.
I am Yours, save me;
for I have sought Your precepts.
The wicked wait for me to destroy me,
but I will consider Your testimonies.
I have seen the consummation of all perfection,
but Your commandment is exceedingly broad.

Knowing and understanding Your Word, O Lord, has helped me in times of trouble. I cannot save my children grief, but I can give them Your weapons to fight despair. I cannot save them tears, but I can give them Your answers that will bring smiles to their faces on the most dismal day.—JB

How Sweet Are Your Promises

Oh, how I love Your law!
It is my meditation all the day.
You, through Your commandments,
make me wiser than my enemies;
for they are ever with me.
I have more understanding
than all my teachers,
for Your testimonies are my meditation.
I understand more than the ancients,
because I keep Your precepts.
I have restrained my feet from
every evil way,
that I may keep Your word.
I have not departed from Your judgments,
for You Yourself have taught me.
How sweet are Your words to my taste,
sweeter than honey to my mouth!
Through Your precepts I get understanding;
therefore I hate every false way.
Your word is a lamp to my feet
and a light to my path.
I have sworn and confirmed
that I will keep Your righteous judgments.
I am afflicted very much;
revive me, O LORD, according to Your word.
Accept, I pray, the freewill offerings
of my mouth, O LORD,
and teach me Your judgments.
My life is continually in my hand,
yet I do not forget Your law....
Your testimonies I have taken as a
heritage forever,
for they are the rejoicing of my heart.
I have inclined my heart to
perform Your statutes
forever, to the very end.

*God's Word is a lamp to my feet for
the immediate, complex,
must-be-answered-now dilemma. It
is also a light for my way to the
murky future. I am blind without it;
I am blessed with it. His word
shines into my life chasing away the
shadows.*—JB

I Stand in Awe of Your Laws

I hate the double-minded, but I love Your law.
You are my hiding place and my shield;
I hope in Your word.
Depart from me, you evildoers,
for I will keep the commandments of my God!
Uphold me according to Your word, that I may live;
and do not let me be ashamed of my hope.
Hold me up, and I shall be safe,
and I shall observe Your statutes continually.
You reject all those who stray from
Your statutes,
for their deceit is falsehood.
You put away all the wicked of the earth like dross;
therefore I love Your testimonies.
My flesh trembles for fear of You,
and I am afraid of Your judgments.
I have done justice and righteousness;
do not leave me to my oppressors.
Be surety for Your servant for good;
do not let the proud oppress me.
My eyes fail from seeking Your salvation
and Your righteous word.
Deal with Your servant according to Your mercy,
and teach me Your statutes.
I am Your servant; give me understanding,
that I may know Your testimonies.
It is time for You to act, O Lord,
for they have regarded Your law as void.
Therefore I love Your commandments
more than gold, yes, than fine gold!
Therefore all Your precepts concerning all things
I consider to be right; I hate every false way.

I have been encouraged to believe that humanity is the measure of all things. I hear constantly that humankind can do all that needs to be done. But I know better, Lord, for no one can hold back the tide or restrain the sun from its allotted purpose. While some may be underwhelmed by Your greatness, I stand awestruck by it and love You for it.—SB

The Entrance of Your Words Gives Light

Your testimonies are wonderful;
therefore my soul keeps them.
The entrance of Your words gives light;
it gives understanding to the simple.
I opened my mouth and panted,
for I longed for Your commandments.
Look upon me and be merciful to me,
as Your custom is toward those who
love Your name.
Direct my steps by Your word,
and let no iniquity have dominion over me.
Redeem me from the oppression of man,
that I may keep Your precepts.
Make Your face shine upon Your servant,
and teach me Your statutes.
Rivers of water run down from my eyes,
because men do not keep Your law.
Righteous are You, O Lord,
and upright are Your judgments.
Your testimonies, which You have commanded,
are righteous and very faithful.
My zeal has consumed me,
because my enemies have forgotten Your words.
Your word is very pure;
therefore Your servant loves it.
I am small and despised,
yet I do not forget Your precepts.
Your righteousness is an everlasting righteousness,
and Your law is truth.
Trouble and anguish have overtaken me,
yet Your commandments are my delights.
The righteousness of Your testimonies
is everlasting;
give me understanding, and I shall live.

From our earliest school days we have run to counselors. We have let others make our decisions for us. We have not learned to make good choices for ourselves. The mighty God and Wonderful Counselor has wise words for us. He will tell us what to do. If we really want to see our way, He will show us!—JB

Your Compassion Is Great, O Lord

I cry out with my whole heart; hear me, O LORD!
I will keep Your statutes.
I cry out to You;
save me, and I will keep Your testimonies.
I rise before the dawning of the morning,
and cry for help; I hope in Your word.
My eyes are awake through the night watches,
that I may meditate on Your word.
Hear my voice according to Your lovingkindness;
O LORD, revive me according to Your justice.
They draw near who follow after wickedness;
they are far from Your law.
You are near, O LORD,
and all Your commandments are truth.
Concerning Your testimonies,
I have known of old that You have
founded them forever.
Consider my affliction and deliver me,
for I do not forget Your law.
Plead my cause and redeem me;
revive me according to Your word.
Salvation is far from the wicked,
for they do not seek Your statutes.
Great are Your tender mercies, O LORD;
revive me according to Your judgments.
Many are my persecutors and my enemies,
yet I do not turn from Your testimonies.
I see the treacherous, and am disgusted,
because they do not keep Your word.
Consider how I love Your precepts;
revive me, O LORD, according to
Your lovingkindness.
The entirety of Your word is truth,
and every one of Your righteous
judgments endures forever.

I find comfort in Your orderliness, Lord. The dawn breaks promptly, the sun runs its race through the heavens at its precise pace. When I meditate on such things, I find relief from the heat of the battle. I enjoy the cool refreshment of Your constancy.—JB

I Have Strayed like a Lost Sheep

Princes persecute me without a cause,
but my heart stands in awe of Your word.
I rejoice at Your word
as one who finds great treasure.
I hate and abhor lying, but I love Your law.
Seven times a day I praise You,
because of Your righteous judgments.
Great peace have those who love
Your law,
and nothing causes them to stumble.
LORD, I hope for Your salvation,
and I do Your commandments.
My soul keeps Your testimonies,
and I love them exceedingly.
I keep Your precepts and Your testimonies,
for all my ways are before You.
Let my cry come before You, O LORD;
give me understanding according to Your word.
Let my supplication come before You;
deliver me according to Your word.
My lips shall utter praise,
for You teach me Your statutes.
My tongue shall speak of Your word,
for all Your commandments are righteousness.
Let Your hand become my help,
for I have chosen Your precepts.
I long for Your salvation, O LORD,
and Your law is my delight.
Let my soul live, and it shall praise You;
and let Your judgments help me.
I have gone astray like a lost sheep;
seek Your servant,
for I do not forget Your commandments.

*People the world over seek after gods of their
own design. But with you, Lord, there is a
difference—You seek after people. I know my
sheeplike propensity to wander, but I rejoice in
your shepherdlike commitment to seek. Even
when I stray, Lord, I really want to be
found.—SB*

I Am a Man of Peace

In my distress I cried to the LORD,
and He heard me.
Deliver my soul, O LORD,
from lying lips
and from a deceitful tongue.
What shall be given to you,
or what shall be done to you,
you false tongue?
Sharp arrows of the warrior,
with coals of the broom tree!
Woe is me, that I sojourn in Meshech,
that I dwell among the tents of Kedar!
My soul has dwelt too long
with one who hates peace.
I am for peace;
but when I speak, they are for war.

*Tolerance lies in seeing in my enemy a person
whom Christ died for. I am called to treat
others as if they are Christ Himself. That is
why I must be a child of peace.*—JB

I Lift My Eyes to the Hills

I will lift up my eyes to the hills—
from whence comes my help?
My help comes from the Lord,
who made heaven and earth.
He will not allow your foot to be moved;
He who keeps you will not slumber.
Behold, He who keeps Israel
shall neither slumber nor sleep.
The Lord is your keeper;
the Lord is your shade at your right hand.
The sun shall not strike you by day,
nor the moon by night.
The Lord shall preserve you from all evil;
He shall preserve your soul.
The Lord shall preserve your going
out and your coming in
from this time forth, and even forevermore.

God has promised to keep me while I sleep; so there does not seem to be too much point in our both staying awake! He has promised to watch over me while I am awake; so there does not seem to be too much point in worrying about my waking hours. As I come and go, He stands still and watches me. That makes me feel very secure!—JB

Our Feet Are Standing in Your Gates, O Jerusalem

I was glad when they said to me,
"Let us go into the house of the LORD."
Our feet have been standing
within your gates, O Jerusalem!
Jerusalem is built
as a city that is compact together,
where the tribes go up, the tribes of the LORD,
to the Testimony of Israel,
to give thanks to the name of the LORD.
For thrones are set there for judgment,
the thrones of the house of David.
Pray for the peace of Jerusalem:
"May they prosper who love you.
Peace be within your walls,
prosperity within your palaces."
For the sake of my brethren and companions,
I will now say, "Peace be within you."
Because of the house of the LORD our God
I will seek your good.

We must take a stand, Lord, and there are so many options. You have something to say on the subject. You have set Your glory in a certain place—You have determined where Your name shall be honored. And we have decided that is where we belong. May Your peace prevail in that place so that our joy might be full.—SB

From the rising of the sun
to its going down
the Lord's name
is to be praised.

The Lord is your keeper;
the Lord is your shade at your right hand.
The sun shall not strike you by day,
nor the moon by night.
The Lord shall preserve you from all evil;
He shall preserve your soul.
The Lord shall preserve your going out
and your coming in from this time forth
and even forevermore.